Table of Contents

Color Bursts

A great way to see how colors combine.

materials

- round coffee filters

- 4 colors of food coloring

- muffin tin

- monofilament line or string

- small clothespins

2

Crafts for Young Children • EMC 720

Steps to follow ➤

1. In the four corners of a muffin tin, mix food coloring with water for the dipping area. (Experiment with the intensity until you are happy with the color the solution makes. Start with four drops of food coloring and one tablespoon of water.)

2. Open the coffee filter flat. Fold it in half several times.

3. Dip each corner of the folded filter into a different food color solution. Do this quickly – the coloring moves very rapidly across the paper.

4. Unfold the filter and dry.

5. Hang the color bursts on the fishing line or string for a cheerful display.

String-Painted Butterflies

This project requires adult assistance, but the lovely creations are worth the extra time.

materials

- template on page 72
- 12" x 18" (30.5 x 45.5 cm) white paper
- 12" x 18" (30.5 x 45.5 cm) colored construction paper
- 3' (9 m) lengths of string
- tempera or poster paints
- Styrofoam meat trays
- paint brush
- hole punch
- 1 yard (1 meter) yarn
- glue

Crafts for Young Children • EMC 720

Steps to follow ▶

1. Cover a table with a plastic paint cloth. Put newspapers on the floor under the painting table. Pour different colors of paint into the meat trays.

2. Fold the large sheet of paper in half. Unfold the paper and lay it near the edge of the table.

3. Dip a length of string into one color of paint. You may want to paint the string with a brush to make sure that it is well coated.

4. Lift the string from the tray and lay it on one side of the white paper. The end should stick out over the edge of the paper.

5. Repeat with several pieces of string dipped into different colors.

6. Fold the paper over the strings. While a helper gently presses down on the top of the folded paper, pull the strings out. Open the paper and let it dry.

7. Refold the paper. Lay the butterfly template on the fold and trace around it. Cut out the butterfly.

8. Lay the butterfly on a 12" x 18" (30.5 x 45.5 cm) colored paper. Cut 1/2" (1.25 cm) away from the butterfly. Glue the butterfly to the backing.

9. Punch a hole and tie yarn to hang the butterfly.

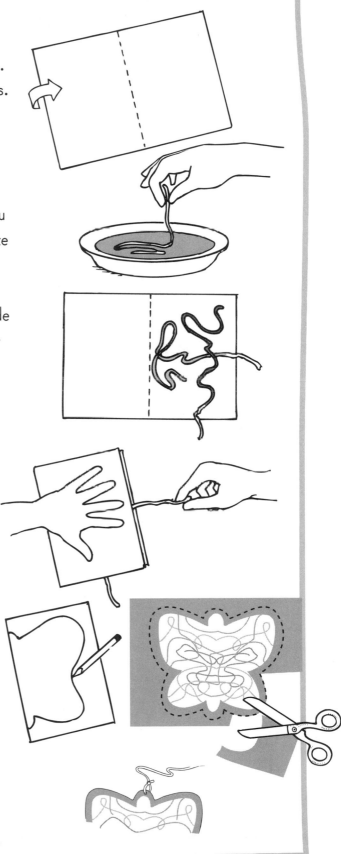

Crafts for Young Children • EMC 720

Magic Pictures

Young artists love to make the hidden shapes appear.

materials

- circles, squares, triangles, or shape patterns on page 7
- tagboard
- 8 1/2" x 11" (21 x 28 cm) white paper
- crayons without wrappers
- 9" x 12" (23 x 30.5 cm) construction paper in a variety of colors.

         Crafts for Young Children • EMC 720

Steps to follow ➤

1. Cut tagboard templates using the patterns on the bottom of this page.

2. Hide several shapes under the white paper.

3. Rub the top of the paper with the side of the unwrapped crayon until the shapes appear.

4. Trim the edges so that the designs take up most of the paper.

5. Mount the magic pictures on colored construction paper.

Variations:

- Use several colors of crayon.
- Use leaves instead of the paper shapes.
- Use bulletin board letters under the paper. Spell a name or word. Cover with the paper. Then rub and read.

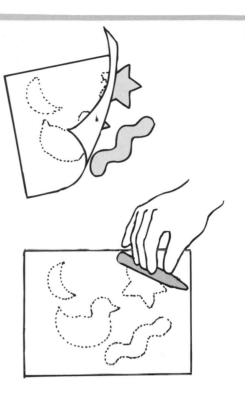

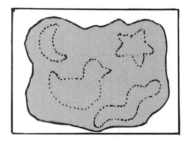

Crafts for Young Children • EMC 720

Buggy Prints

Make a bug walking across a paper hand.

materials

- poster paint
- pencil with an eraser
- 6" (11.5 x 15 cm) square of white paper
- 9" (23 cm) square of colored construction paper
- fine-tip black pen

Steps to follow ➤

1. Trace child's hand on paper. Cut it out.

2. Dip the eraser end of the pencil into the
   paint and press the painty eraser onto the
   paper hand.
   - Make three prints close together
   for a bug's body.
   - Make six or seven prints for a
   caterpillar.

3. Let the paint dry and then add legs and
   antennae with the black pen.

4. Glue the hand to a colored paper square.

Crayon Resist Sailboats

Use watercolor washes to accent these crayon drawings.

materials

- 9" x 12" (23 x 30.5) white drawing paper
- crayons
- watercolor paints
- containers for water

Crafts for Young Children • EMC 720

Steps to follow ➤

Drawing the Picture

1. Direct the drawing of a sailboat. You draw on the chalkboard, a chart, or the overhead projector. Students do each step as you demonstrate. Encourage them to draw large, filling the paper. When they color in the shapes, stress pressing hard to make the crayon quite dark.

   • Draw a triangle in the middle of your paper with a black crayon.

   • Leave some space and add the bottom of the boat.

   • Add the mast to hold up the sail.

   • There might be a small triangular flag flying from the top of the mast.

   • Color the sail, the boat, and the flag.

   • Add some waves, clouds in the sky, and a few sea gulls.

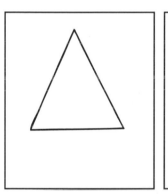 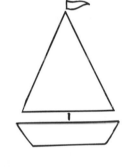 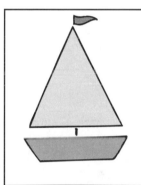 

The Water Color Wash

1. Cover a table with a plastic paint cloth. Set sailboat pictures on the covered table.

2. Wet the brush and dip it into the watercolor pan. Brush across the picture of the sailboats. You may want to use one color for the sky and one color for the water.

3. Allow the picture to dry.

Tube Printing

Here's another way to paint without a brush.

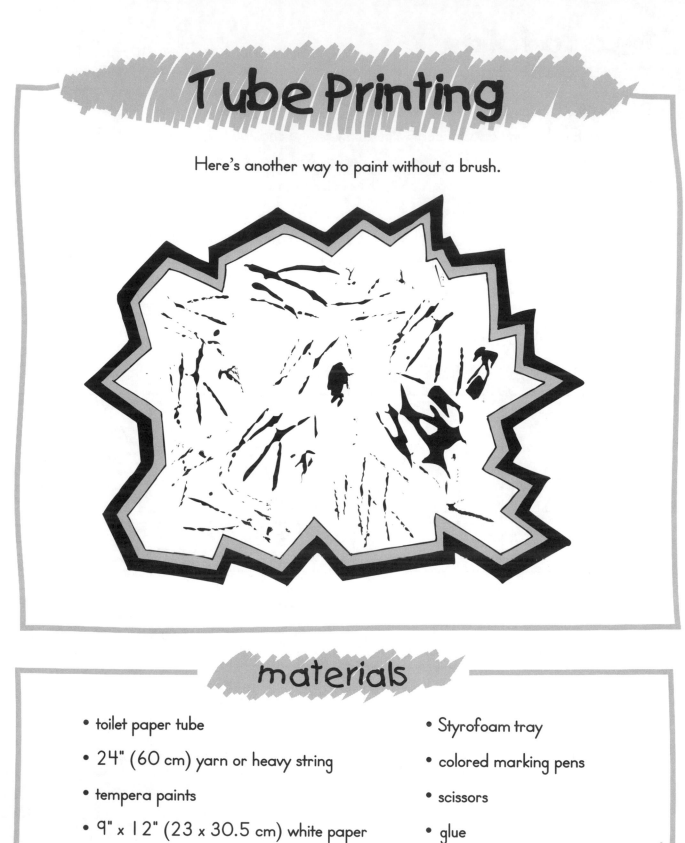

materials

- toilet paper tube
- 24" (60 cm) yarn or heavy string
- tempera paints
- 9" x 12" (23 x 30.5 cm) white paper
- 9" x 12" (23 x 30.5 cm) colored construction paper

- Styrofoam tray
- colored marking pens
- scissors
- glue

Steps to follow ⟩

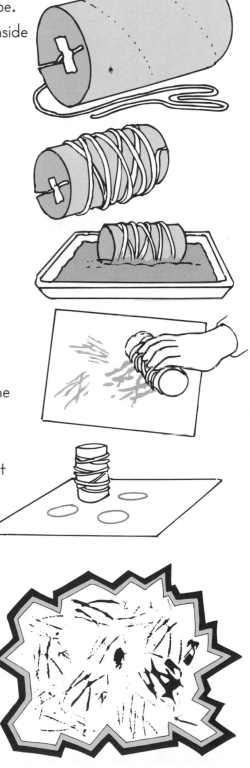

Making the Tube

You may want an adult to do most of this phase.

1. Make a short slit on the edge of the toilet paper tube. Stick the end of string through the slit and tape it inside the tube.

2. Wrap the string around the tube. Secure the other end of the string at the other end of the tube.

Printing

1. Cover the work area with a plastic paint cloth.

2. Pour some paint on the Styrofoam tray. Dip a section of the tube in the paint.

3. Roll the tube over the paper. Repeat several times.

4. Dip the end of the tube in the paint and press on the paper. Repeat several times. Let dry.

Variation: Use several colors of paint, being sure to let each color dry before adding the next color.

Framing the Print

1. Have an adult draw an interesting outline around the print with a marking pen the same color as the paint used.

2. Let students cut along this outline.

3. Glue the print to contrasting construction paper.

Baker's Clay Snail

Baker's clay is great for rolling and cutting with cookie cutters.
It is very flexible and holds its shape well.

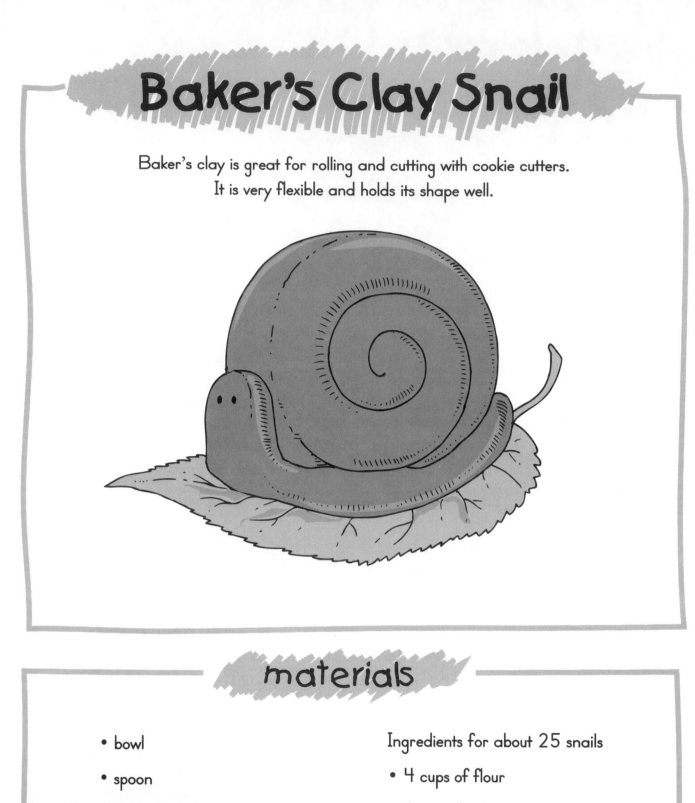

materials

- bowl

- spoon

- cookie sheet

- small containers of water

- real leaves

Ingredients for about 25 snails

- 4 cups of flour

- 1 cup of salt

- 1 1/2 cups of warm water

   Crafts for Young Children • EMC 720

Steps to follow ➤

Making the Clay

1. Dissolve the salt in the warm water.

2. Stir in the flour.

3. Knead the dough for at least five minutes.

Note: Keep the clay in a plastic bag so it will not dry out.

Forming the Snail

1. Give each student 2 walnut-sized balls of clay.

2. Roll one ball into a long "snake."

3. Form the "snake" into a coil for the snail shell.

4. Roll the other ball into a flat tube to form the snail's body.

5. Moisten the bottom of the "shell" and the center of the "body" with water. Set the "shell" on the "body" and press gently to attach.

6. Roll the "head" up. Poke 2 holes for eyes with a pencil point.

7. Bake the snails in a 300° oven until hard.

8. Set each snail on a real leaf to carry home.

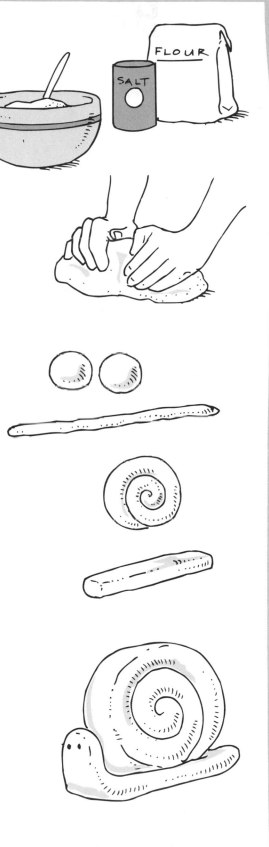

Cornstarch Clay Penguin

Cornstarch clay is a pure white clay. It will air dry in several days and can be baked in the oven at low temperatures if you want it to harden more quickly.

materials

- saucepan

- stove top or hot plate

- spoon

- cutting board

- cookie sheet

- black, white, yellow tempera paint

- paint brushes

- cotton swabs

Ingredients for 10–15 penguins

- 1 cup cornstarch

- 2 cups baking soda

- 1 1/3 cup water

Crafts for Young Children • EMC 720

Steps to follow ▶

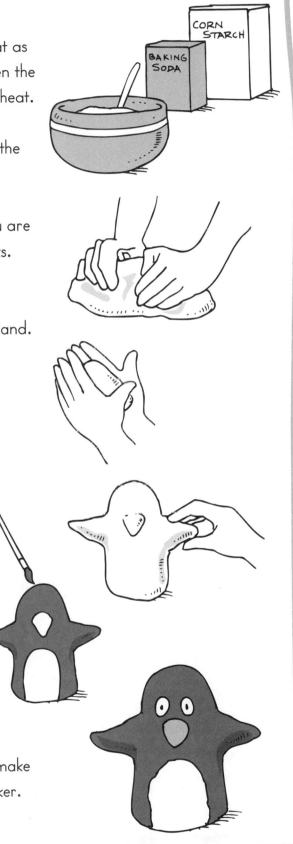

Making the Clay

1. Put the water into a pan. Stir over medium heat as you add the cornstarch and baking soda. When the mixture is like mashed potatoes remove it from heat.

2. Pour onto a cutting board to cool. As soon as the dough is cool enough, knead it.

3. Keep the clay in an airtight container when you are not working with it. It will keep for several weeks.

Forming the Penguin

1. Roll a 2" (5cm) diameter ball of clay in your hand.

2. Shape it into a fat log.

3. Pinch a beak out of the front of the log.

4. Pinch a wing out of each side.

5. Let the penguin dry or bake it until it's hard in a 300° oven.

Painting the Penguin

1. Paint the penguin black. Let dry.

2. Dip a thumb in thick white paint to "paint" penguin's tummy.

3. Dip the tip of a cotton swab in white paint to make eyes. When dry add the pupil with black marker.

4. Paint the penguin's beak yellow.

     Crafts for Young Children • EMC 720

Crepe Paper Clay Bowl

Crepe paper clay will be the color of the crepe paper that you use.
Don't mix colors unless you want a gray tone. This "clay" has a bumpy texture.

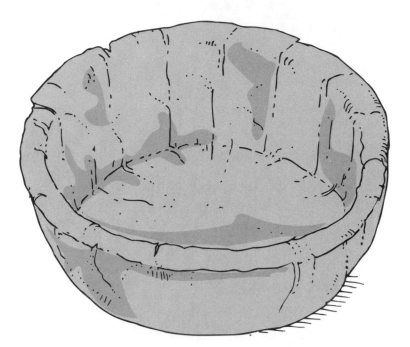

materials

- mixing bowl

- spoon

- plastic glasses or plastic
  1/2 cup measuring cups
  for molding forms

- plastic wrap

- sand paper

- gloss finish

- paint brushes

Ingredients for one bowl

- 1 cup crepe paper

- 1 cup warm water

- 1/2 to 2/3 cup flour

- 2 teaspoons salt

Steps to follow ➤

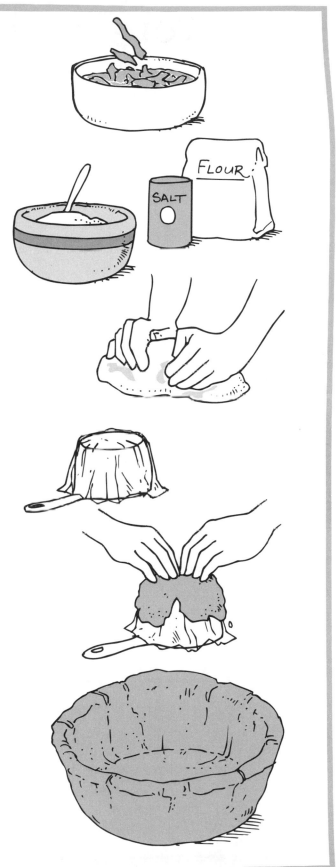

Making the Clay

1. Tear the crepe paper into tiny pieces. Put the pieces of paper in a bowl and cover them with warm water.

2. Wait several hours. Pour off the water.

3. Mix the flour and salt together and add the flour mixture to the wet paper gradually, stirring as you go. Stop adding flour when the clay is stiff.

4. Knead until the clay is pliable.

Making the Bowl

1. Cover a small glass or measuring cup with plastic wrap.

2. Pat the crepe paper clay over the bowl. Make a thick layer. Smooth the edges.

3. Let the clay dry for several days.

4. Remove the bowl and the plastic wrap. Sand the edges of the clay bowl if they are rough.

5. Brush or spray on a gloss finish.

A Caterpillar from a Sock

Children will be delighted with this "squishy" toy.

materials

- a tube sock (The size of your caterpillar will depend on the size of your sock.)

- plastic grocery bags

- felt scraps

- buttons or wiggly eyes

- 1 yard (1 meter) pieces of yarn

- rubber bands

- glue

- red fabric marking pens

Crafts for Young Children • EMC 720

Steps to follow ▶

1. Cut the ribbing off the tube sock. Turn the sock inside out.

2. Stuff the sock with plastic grocery bags.

3. Wrap a rubber band around the open end to close it.

4. Wrap rubber bands around the sock to create the segments of the caterpillar's body.

5. Cut two circles of felt for the eyes. Glue the eyes to the caterpillar. Glue buttons or wiggly eyes on top of the felt eyes.

6. Draw a happy mouth with marking pen.

7. Tie a piece of yarn around the first segment rubber band to make a leash. Take your caterpillar for a walk.

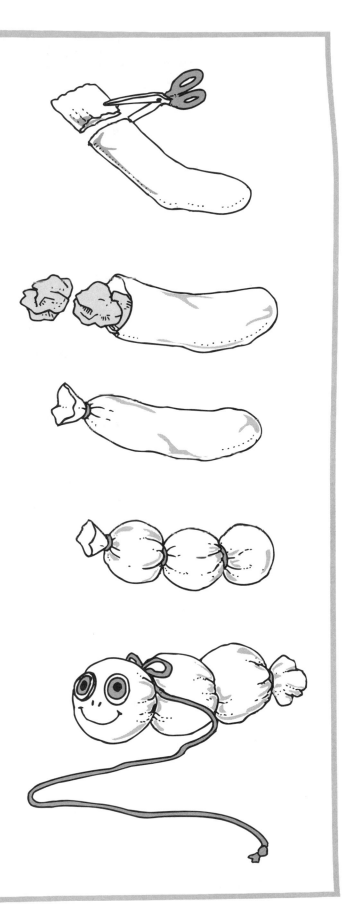

A Sun Collage

Create your own sun to brighten a cloudy day.

materials

- 9" (23 cm) corrugated cardboard square

- white glue

- several different kinds of noodles

- gold spray paint

Crafts for Young Children • EMC 720

Steps to follow ➤

1. Trace around a circular shape (the bottom of a jar, a flower pot, a pencil holder, a glass, etc.) on the cardboard to form the face of the sun.

2. Cover a small area with white glue and press the noodles into glue. Repeat until the circle is full.

3. Add the sun's rays with more noodles.

4. When the collage is dry, spray it with gold paint. (An adult should do this step.)

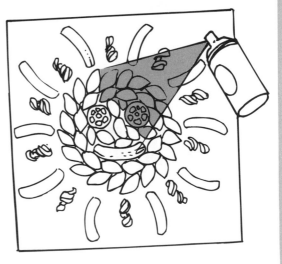

Crafts for Young Children • EMC 720

Beautiful Butterfly

Hang these butterflies from your ceiling with fishing line
and they will look like they're really flying.

materials

- brightly colored 1" (2.5 cm) wide
  construction paper strips
    - 2 – 14" (35.5 cm)
    - 2 – 10" (25.5 cm)
    - 2 – 6" (15 cm)

- toilet paper roll

- 2 large headed paper fasteners
- 1 pipe cleaner
- tempera paint
- glue
- hole punch
- wiggly eyes
- clothespin

Steps to follow ▶

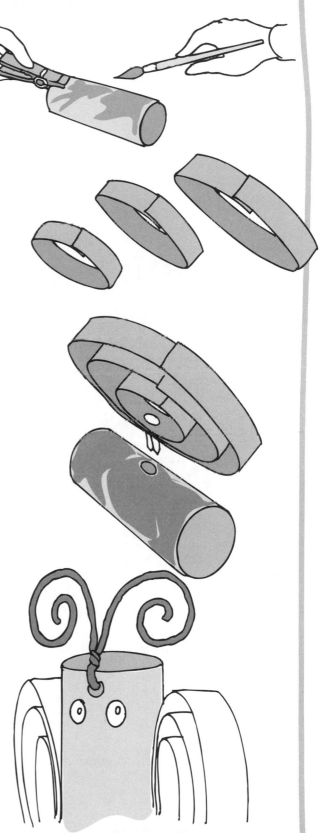

Body

1. Hold paper tube with a clothespin as you paint it.

2. Let tube dry.

Wings

1. Glue ends of each strip of paper together to form a ring. Hold closed until glue begins to set.

2. Punch a hole in each ring.

3. Lay a small- and medium-sized ring inside the largest ring, lining up punched holes.

4. Put the paper fastener through the holes, and then poke it through the side of the paper tube, opening the tines inside the tube.

5. Repeat steps 3 and 4 to make the other wing.

Finishing Details

1. Punch a hole near the top center of the paper tube.

2. Run the pipe cleaner through the hole. Twist it around itself to secure it, and curl the ends to form antennae.

3. Glue on wiggly eyes below the punched hole.

                   Crafts for Young Children • EMC 720

Rainbow Sparkle Mobile

A tiny bit of glitter turns a circle, a square, and a triangle into sparkling shapes.

materials

- glitter and tiny sequins
- clear contact paper
- string
- manila–colored tag board
- rainbow pattern and shape templates on page 73
- marking pens
- scissors
- yarn
- hole punch

Crafts for Young Children • EMC 720

Steps to follow ➤

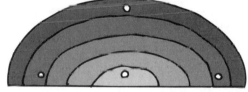

Make Glitter Paper

1. Lay a piece of clear contact paper, sticky side up, in the lid of a box.

2. Let students help to sprinkle pinches of glitter and tiny sequins on the paper. (Don't use too much glitter or the contact paper will not stick.)

3. Cover the paper with a second piece of contact paper, sticky side down.

4. You will need a 10" x 4" (25.5 x 10 cm) piece of glitter paper for each student.

Hanger

1. Provide each student with a tagboard hanger made by using the pattern on page 73. More capable groups can cut out the shape that you have traced onto the tagboard.

2. Color the rainbow pattern with markers, cut out, and glue to the tagboard.

Glitter Shapes

1. Make tagboard templates from the shape patterns on page 73. Depending on the age and ability of the group, you can let students trace around the templates onto the glitter paper, or you can outline the shapes for them.

3. Cut a circle, a square, and a triangle from the glitter paper.

Making the Mobile

1. Punch a hole in each shape and at the places indicated on the rainbow.

3. Tie a piece of yarn to each shape and then to the rainbow hanger.

Variation

Add a few clouds cut from white construction paper.

Bunny Cup

Create this cute bunny using a paper cup.

materials

- white paper cup (no wax coating)

- scraps of construction paper, poster board, or foamies

- black marking pen

- colored marking pens

- cotton balls

- glue

Steps to follow ❯

1. Make a template to trace using the ear pattern below.

2. Trace the ear piece on the construction paper, poster board, or foamy. Cut it out.

3. Have an adult make a slit across the paper cup's base.

4. Slip the ear piece into the slit.

5. Draw eyes, nose, cheeks, and mouth on the cup.

6. Glue a cotton "tail" to the back.

A Hairy Egg Head

Plant grass seeds in egg shells to create these funny characters.

materials

- empty egg shell half
- potting soil
- grass seed
- permanent markers for face
- colored marking pens
- egg carton
- toilet paper tube
- construction paper scraps
- 4" (10 cm) construction paper squares

Steps to follow ➤

Making the Head

1. Draw a face on the egg shell half with the markers. (The broken edge should face up.)

2. Carefully spoon soil into the shell. Fill it 1/2 full.

3. Sprinkle grass seed over the soil. Cover with another spoonful of soil.

4. Put shells in an open egg carton on a window sill. Allow a week for the grass to sprout and grow. Water the tiny garden as needed.

Making the Body

1. Use the construction paper scraps and/or marking pens to decorate the paper tube to resemble a person (shirt, pants, dress, uniform, etc.).

2. Dip one round edge of the paper tube in glue and set it on the construction paper square. This will keep the tube from tipping over.

3. When the grass is growing well, balance the head in the top of the body tube. You may need to give your hairy egg head a haircut if its hair grows out of control!

Buddy Bear

This bear can hang or sit to cheer up any room. Sit him on your lap while you share bear stories and poems.

materials

- patterns and templates on page 74
- 9" x 12" (23 x 30.5 cm) brown construction paper
- pink paper

- 2 paper fasteners
- crayons
- glue
- scissors
- heart stickers

Crafts for Young Children • EMC 720

Steps to follow ➤

1. Cut brown paper in half. Use one half for bear body. On the other half, trace and cut arms and ears using templates on page 74.

2. Cut halfway up the center of the body to make legs.

3. Color and cut out one of the face patterns on page 74.

4. Glue face and ears to body.

5. Attach arms with paper fasteners.

6. Cut pink paper half circles for paws.

7. Add a heart sticker to your bear.

         Crafts for Young Children • EMC 720

School of Fish

Let these fish "swim" across a blue bulletin board on which you've stapled sea plants and perhaps a sunken treasure chest.

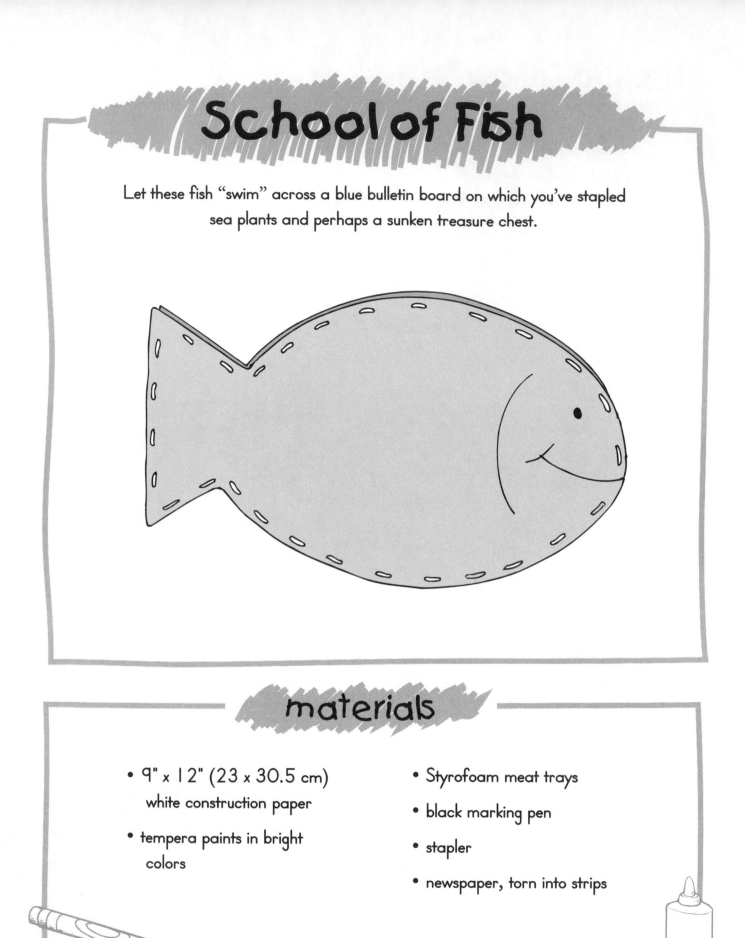

materials

- 9" x 12" (23 x 30.5 cm) white construction paper

- tempera paints in bright colors

- Styrofoam meat trays

- black marking pen

- stapler

- newspaper, torn into strips

Steps to follow ⟩

1. Cut the construction paper into a fish shape. Each child will need 2.

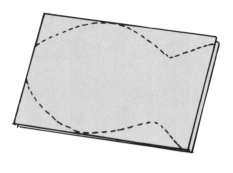

2. Add eyes, mouth, and gill slit to both pieces with marking pen.

3. Press thumb into paint and print scales on the fish. Let dry.

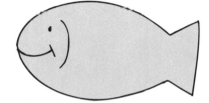

4. Staple 2 fish patterns together around the edge, leaving an opening for stuffing.

5. Stuff fish with newspaper and staple shut.

Magic Wand

Perfect for a fairy princess or a magician!

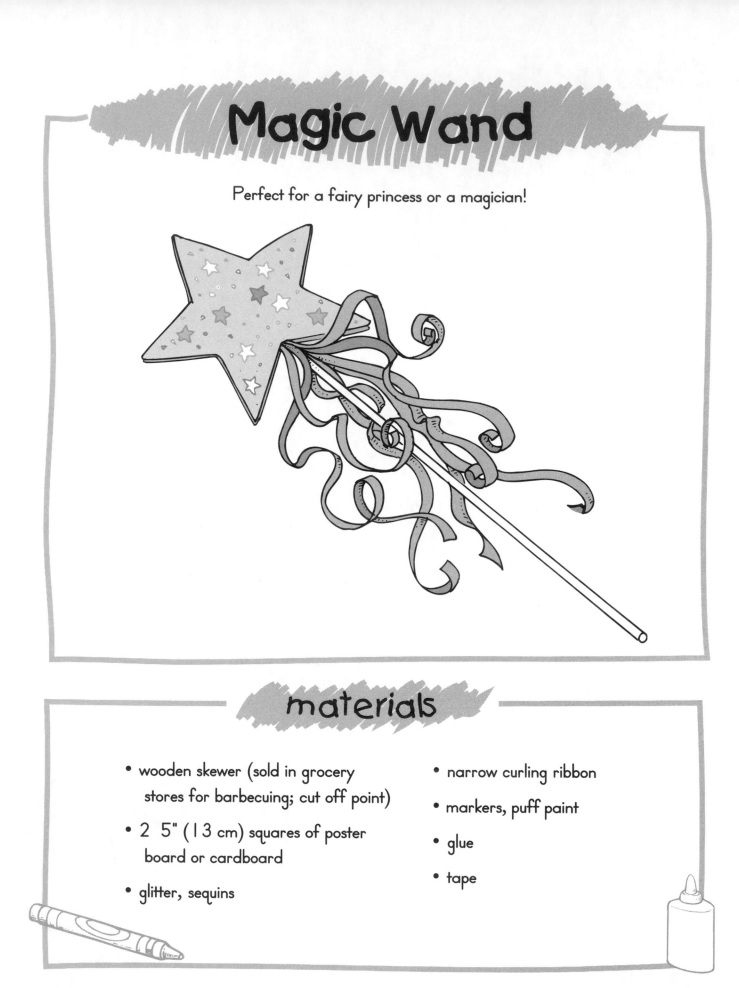

- wooden skewer (sold in grocery stores for barbecuing; cut off point)

- 2 5" (13 cm) squares of poster board or cardboard

- glitter, sequins

- narrow curling ribbon

- markers, puff paint

- glue

- tape

Steps to follow ➤

1. Prepare a star tracer using the pattern on the bottom of this page.

2. Trace the star onto the two squares and cut them out. (Note: If your poster board is colored on only one side, trace the star on one square, colored side up. Cut out the star. Lay the newly cut star on the plain side of the second square—color side down. Trace and cut out the second star.)

3. Decorate your star with glitter, markers, puff paint, and sequins.

4. Tape one end of the skewer to the back of one of the stars.

5. Tape several strands of ribbon near the base of the same star. Curl the ends gently.

6. Glue the second star on top of the first star. Let it dry completely.

An Octopus for your Bath

, This octopus is a lot more fun than a washcloth.
Buy the foam for this project at any fabric store.

materials

- 1/4" (64 mm) foam –
  1 yd (1 meter) will make 4 octopuses

- waterproof glue

- permanent marking pens

38

Steps to follow ➤

1. Cut foam in 12" x 9" (30.5 x 23 cm) sections. Cut two body shapes as shown.

2. Cut up halfway for tentacles. If desired, cut the tentacles to points.

3. Glue the two shapes together as shown.

4. Draw a face and add the suction cups on back sides of the legs.

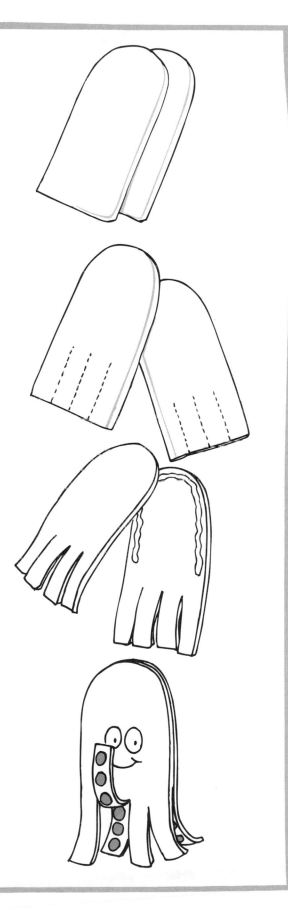

A Rattle Tube

Use your rattle stick to accompany your favorite songs.

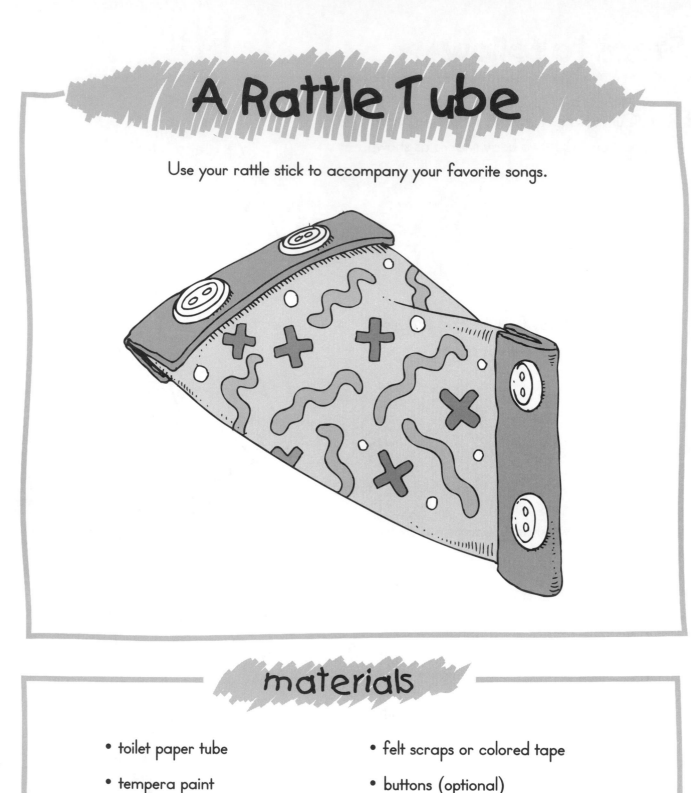

materials

- toilet paper tube

- tempera paint

- paint brushes

- beans or pebbles

- felt scraps or colored tape

- buttons (optional)

- stapler

Crafts for Young Children • EMC 720

Steps to follow ➤

1. Paint the paper tube. Let it dry completely.

2. Staple one end of the tube closed.

3. Put a small handful of beans or pebbles into the tube.

4. Turn the tube a quarter turn and staple the other end closed. One end will have a horizontal closure and one end will have a vertical closure.

5. Cover the two stapled ends with strips of felt or colored tape.

6. Decorate the rattle – glue buttons to the felt strips, put designs on the tube with marking pens, add stickers, glitter, etc.

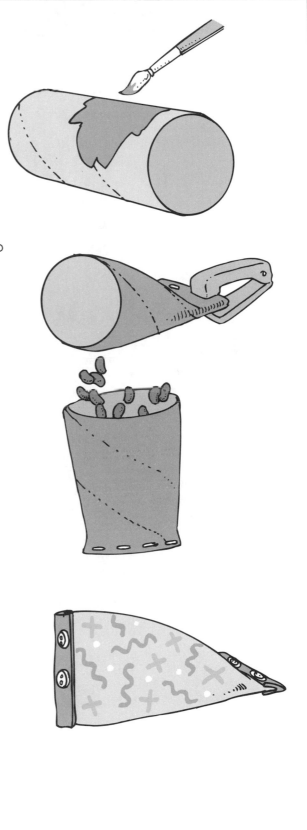

Crafts for Young Children • EMC 720

Finger Puppets

Create several puppets and then enjoy the conversations between them.
A table turned on its side makes a great puppet theater.

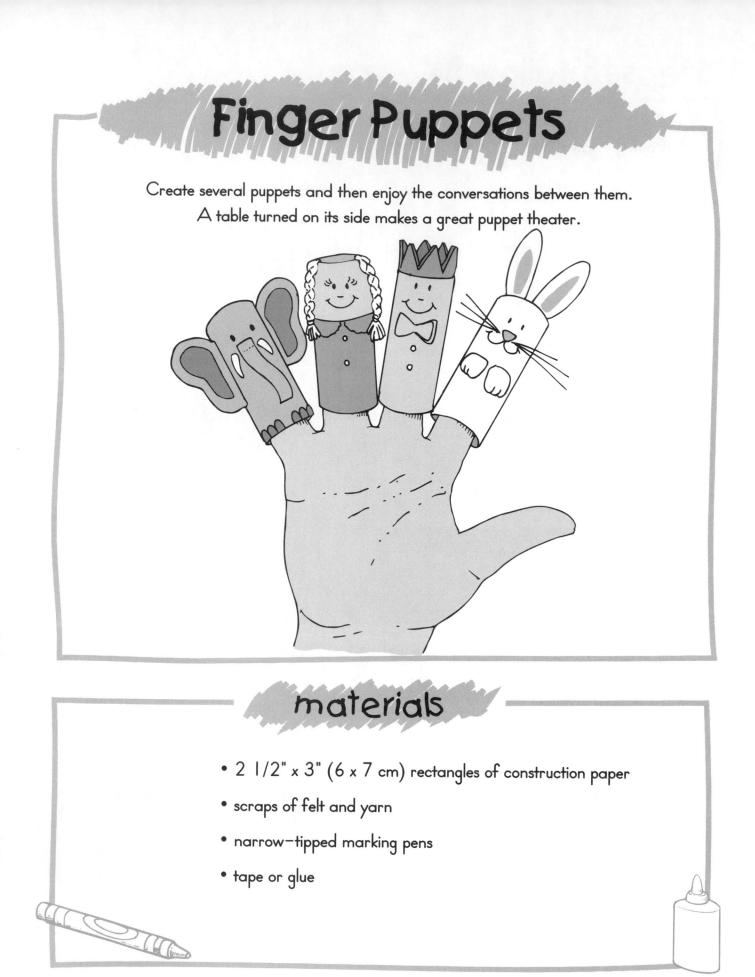

materials

- 2 1/2" x 3" (6 x 7 cm) rectangles of construction paper
- scraps of felt and yarn
- narrow–tipped marking pens
- tape or glue

Crafts for Young Children • EMC 720

Steps to follow ⟩

1. Roll the paper rectangle into a tube and secure with tape or glue.

2. Draw a face on the side that is not taped.

3. Add felt and yarn as desired to create funny people, animals, and imaginary creatures.

Origami Mouse

This mouse is a good folding experience for young fingers.

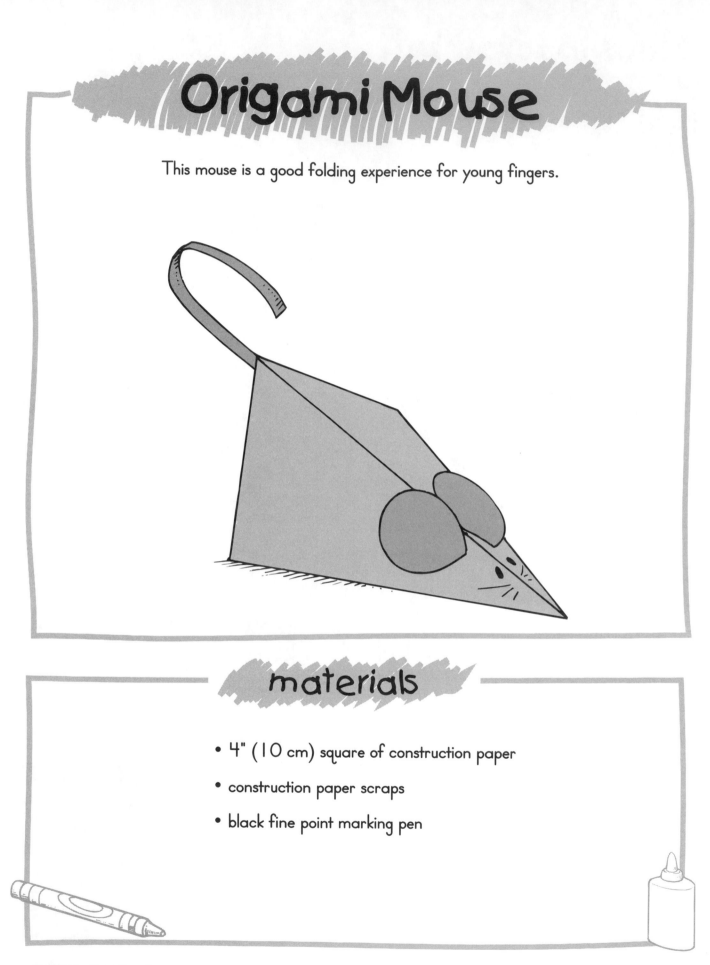

materials

- 4" (10 cm) square of construction paper

- construction paper scraps

- black fine point marking pen

Steps to follow ➤

1. Fold the paper square in half diagonally.

2. Unfold the square.

3. Make a kite shape. Lay the square in front of you so that it looks like a diamond. The line from the fold should point at your stomach. Fold the corner on your left to the center fold line. Fold the corner on your right to the center fold line.

4. Fold the kite shape in half along the diagonal so that the flaps are inside.

5. Open the fold so that a tiny tent forms. The two flaps will overlap at the bottom of the tent. Glue the overlapping flaps together.

6. Cut the scraps of paper to make ears and a tail for your mouse. Glue them on to the mouse. Draw eyes with marking pen.

Variation:
Vary the size of the square and create a whole family of mice!

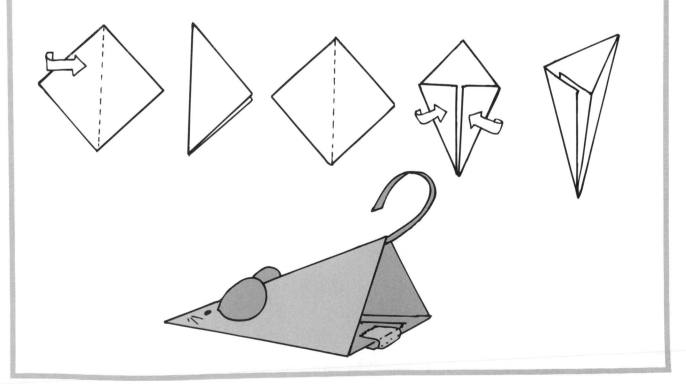

A Pie Pan Mobile

Take a walk and collect nature's treasures to hang on your mobile.

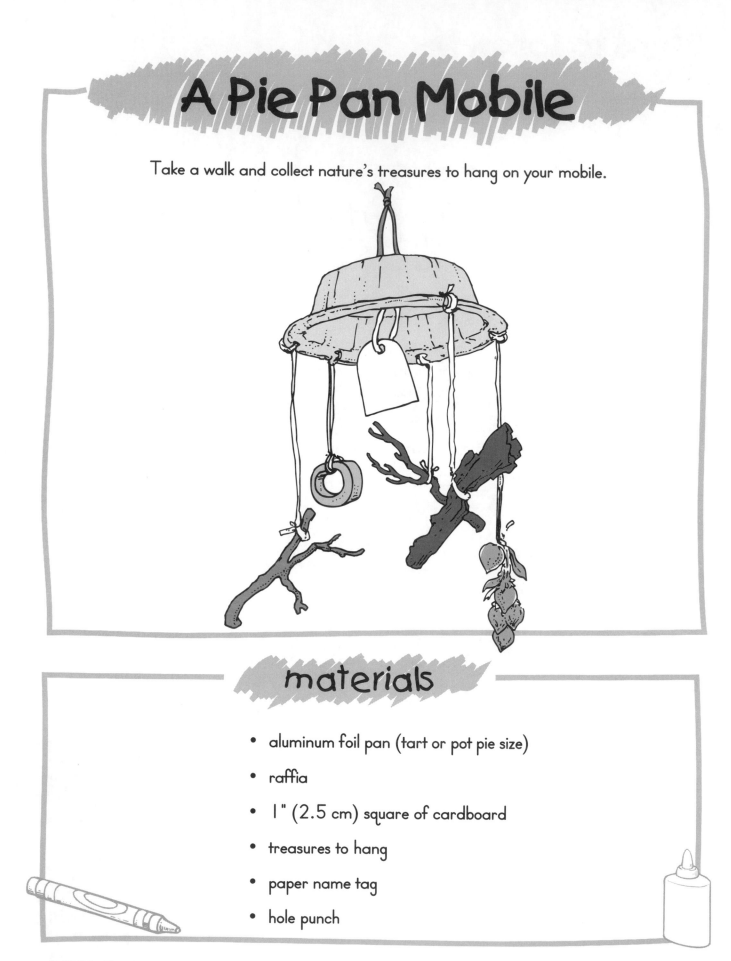

materials

- aluminum foil pan (tart or pot pie size)

- raffia

- 1" (2.5 cm) square of cardboard

- treasures to hang

- paper name tag

- hole punch

46   Crafts for Young Children • EMC 720

Steps to follow >

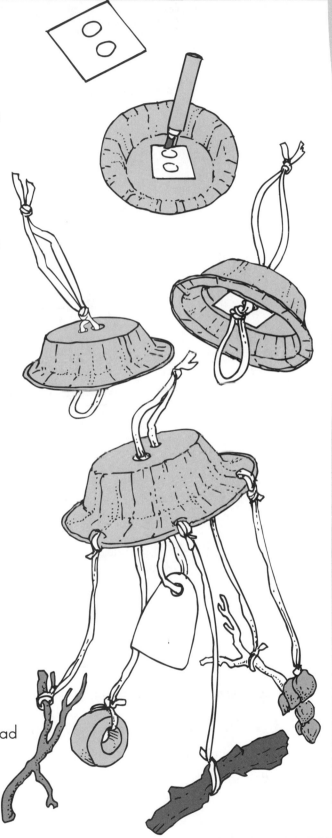

1. Punch two holes in the cardboard square.

2. Center the cardboard square inside the pan. Mark the spots where the holes are. Have an adult poke two holes in the pie pan where the marks are.

3. Thread a 12" (30 cm) piece of raffia down through the one hole in the pan and the cardboard square and back up through the other hole.

   Tie the raffia together close to the pan and then again at the end to create a hanging loop. (Using the cardboard square will prevent the aluminum foil from tearing when you hang your mobile.)

4. Punch holes at even distances around the edge of the pan.

5. Put raffia through each hole.

6. Tie treasures to the raffia pieces.

7. Punch a hole in the name tag, and thread a piece of raffia through the hole. Pass the raffia under the loop on the inside center of the pan and knot.

An Easy Reindeer

Make these reindeer in different sizes for decorations.

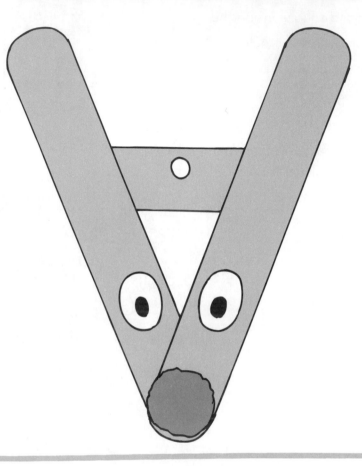

materials

- three strips of brown construction paper (see pattern on page 49)

- 1 1/2" (4 cm) red or black pompon (felt, fleece or paper circles may be substituted)

- 2 wiggly eyes or white and black construction paper scraps

- yarn

- hole punch

- glue

Crafts for Young Children • EMC 720

Steps to follow ➤

1. Trace the patterns below on brown construction paper. Cut out the strips.

2. Make a "V" with the two large strips. Glue the tip of the "V" together.

3. Place the small strip across the middle of the "V." Glue it to each side of the "V."

5. Glue on pompon nose and wiggly eyes (or cut circles from paper or fabric and glue on).

6. Punch a hole on the cross piece for hanging the reindeer.

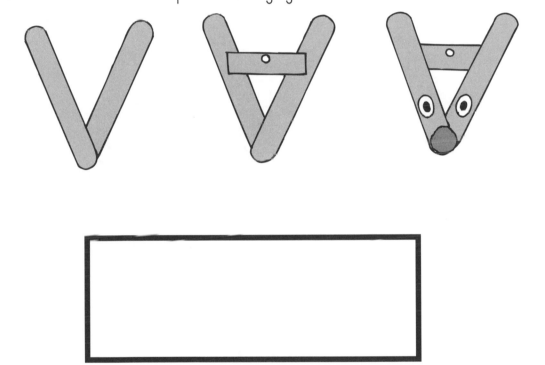

Racing Bugs

Egg carton bugs are fun to race on any slope. Watch them spin out at the end of the run.

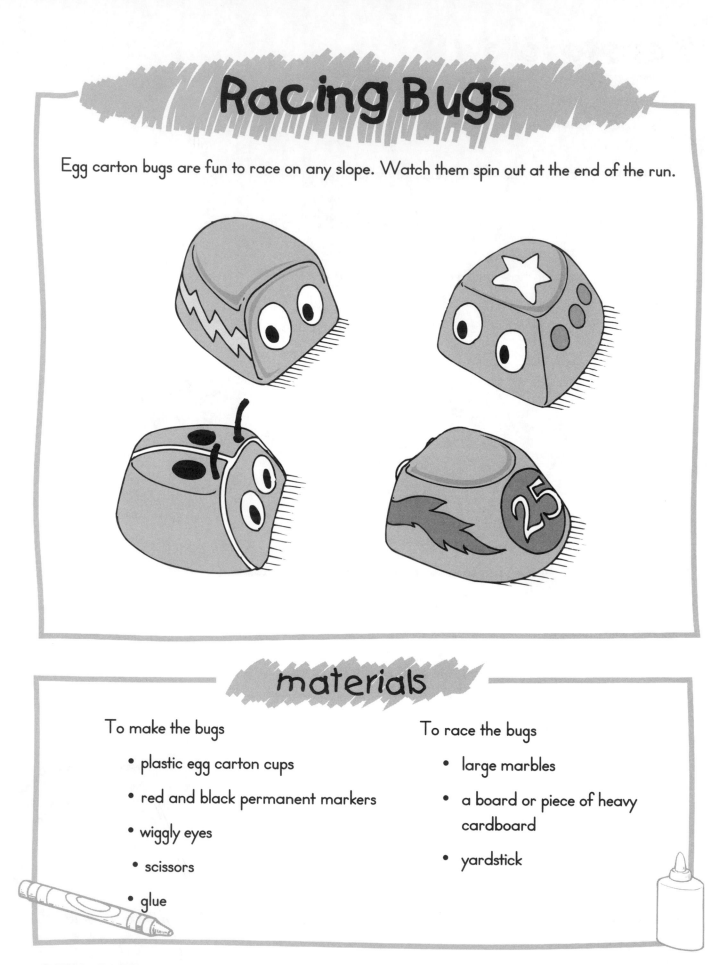

materials

To make the bugs

- plastic egg carton cups
- red and black permanent markers
- wiggly eyes
- scissors
- glue

To race the bugs

- large marbles
- a board or piece of heavy cardboard
- yardstick

Crafts for Young Children • EMC 720

Steps to follow ▶

Make a Bug

1. Trim the cup portion of an egg carton so that the edges are smooth.

2. Color the cup with permanent marker or paint.

3. Glue two wiggly eyes to the front.

Racing the Bugs

1. Create a smooth slope with a board or heavy cardboard. Experiment to find the degree of slope that works best for you.

2. The starter will hold a yardstick at the top of the slope.

3. Each child places a marble behind the yardstick and covers the marble with the bug.

4. The starter begins the race by raising the yardstick and the bugs race to the finish line.

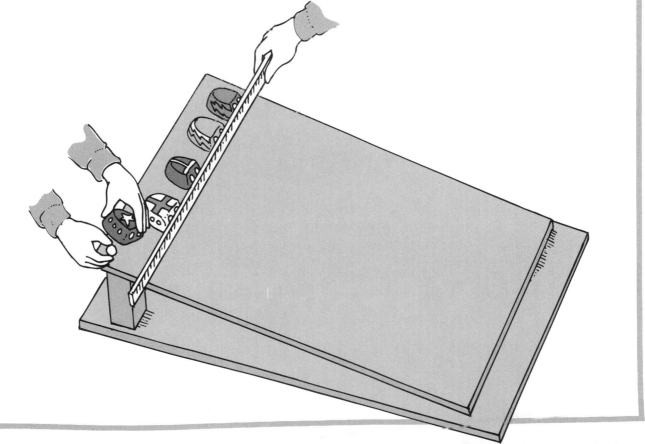

Nest Supply Storehouse

Help birds to find the supplies that they need for their nests by building a nest supply storehouse. Hang it outside in a tree and then keep it well stocked.

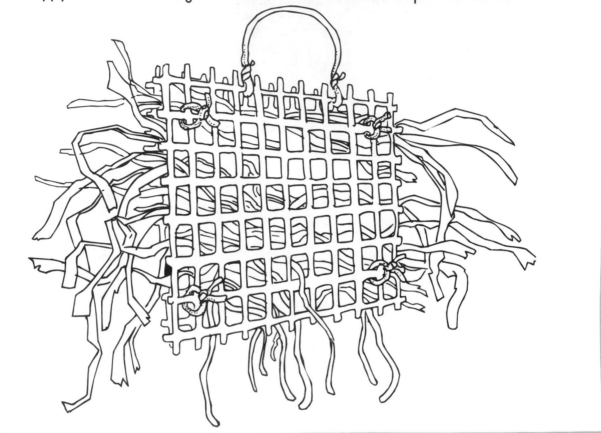

materials

- 2 5" (13 cm) squares of mesh (wire mesh or plastic canvas)

- twist ties

- bird nest supplies — string, yarn, fabric scraps, dryer lint, raffia, etc.

 Crafts for Young Children • EMC 720

Steps to follow ➤

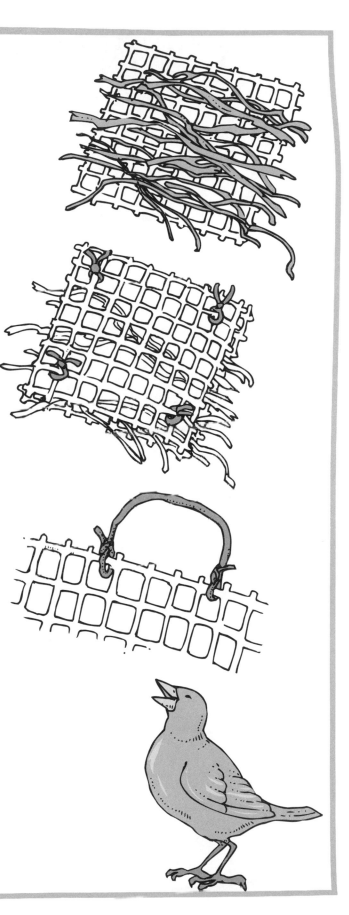

1. Lay one square of mesh on the table.

2. Cover the mesh square with nesting supplies.

3. Lay the other square of mesh on top of the supplies. Press it down and attach it at the four corners with twist ties. (Two pairs of hands make this job much easier.)

4. Make a hanging loop with another twist lie.

5. Find a low branch and hang your storehouse.

             Crafts for Young Children • EMC 720

A Bead Pin

This exercise in patterning becomes wearable art.

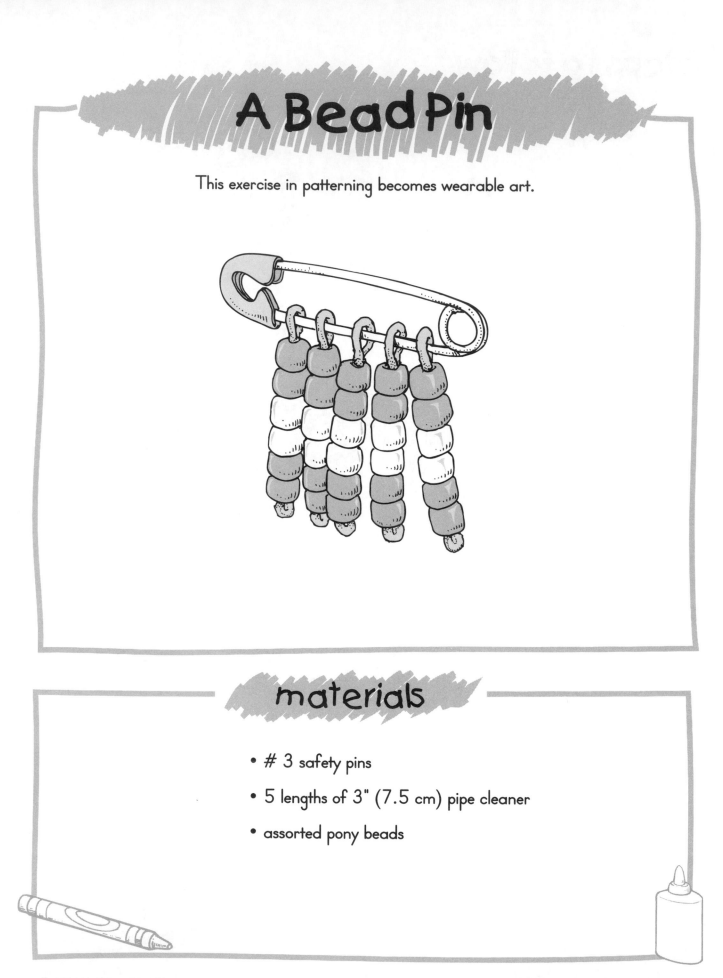

materials

- # 3 safety pins
- 5 lengths of 3" (7.5 cm) pipe cleaner
- assorted pony beads

Crafts for Young Children • EMC 720

Steps to follow >

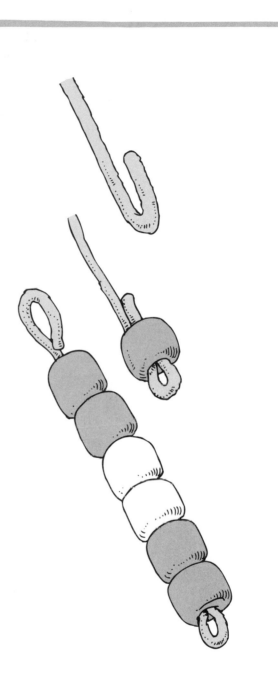

1. Loop over one end of a pipe cleaner. Squeeze the loop against the length of pipe cleaner.

2. Decide on a pattern to make from 6 pony beads.

3. Slip on the first bead and push it down over the double section of pipe cleaner.

4. When the six–bead pattern is complete, secure the beads by bending up the other end of the pipe cleaner.

5. Repeat four more times, making the same bead pattern each time. Slip all 5 pipe cleaners onto the open safety pin. Pin it to your shirt and show off your work.

Sew a Picture

Yarn, ribbon, and string in combinations make attractive sewn pictures.

materials

- 7" (18 cm) tagboard circles

- 2' (61 cm) lengths of colorful, shiny ribbon, yarn, and string in assorted colors and widths

- cellophane tape

- hole punch

- feathers (optional)

Steps to follow ▶

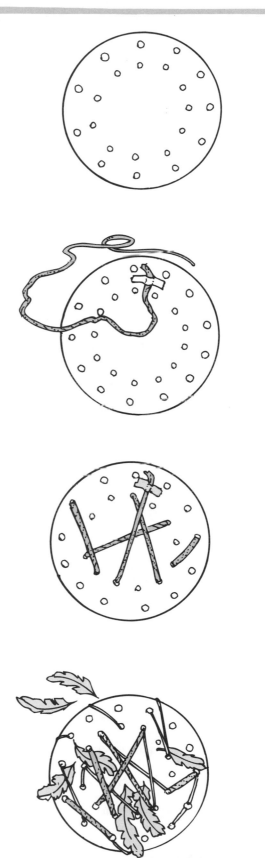

1. Prepare the sewing cards. Cut out tagboard circles and punch a series of holes around the edge.

2. Tape the end of a 2 foot (61 cm) piece of yarn or ribbon to the edge of the sewing card. (Knots are too hard for little fingers. Taping solves the problem.)

3. Sew by going from hole to hole in a random pattern. The design will be most effective if you cross wider spaces rather than going to nearby holes.

4. When you reach the end of the yarn, tape it and begin again with another color and/or type of yarn or ribbon.

Note: A small piece of tape around the end of the yarn will keep it from unraveling as you sew with it.

5. Finish your creation by weaving feathers through the sewn design.

A Box Puzzle

What a fun way to create a collection of puzzles to enjoy!

materials

- 4 small JELL-O® boxes
- spray paint
- glue
- patterns on page 75-77
- cellophane tape

Students need two drawings in order to create a puzzle on both sides of the boxes.
Page 75 is a blank template so that students can draw their own pictures.
Pages 76 & 77 provide pictures for students to color.

Steps to follow ➤

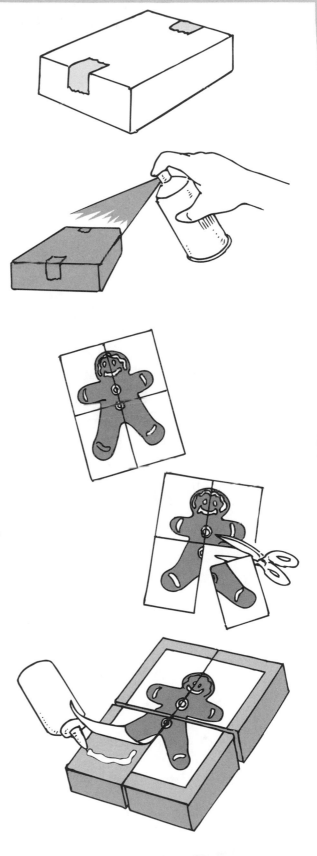

Preparing the Boxes

1. Tape the empty boxes closed.

2. Spray paint the boxes on all sides. Let them dry completely.

Making a Puzzle

1. Color two pictures using the patterns on pages 75–77.

2. Cut the pictures apart on the lines.

3. Lay the boxes out to create a square.

4. Lay one drawing on the boxes so that the picture pieces fit together.

5. Glue the drawing to the boxes.

6. Turn the boxes over and repeat with another drawing.

     Crafts for Young Children • EMC 720

Framed Family Portrait

Show off these family portraits with an easy three-dimensional frame.

materials

- 3" x 6" (7.5 x 15 cm) white drawing paper
- 6" x 9" (15 x 23 cm) colored construction paper
- crayons or marking pens
- glue
- pinking shears

Crafts for Young Children • EMC 720

Steps to follow >

1. Have children draw their families on the white paper.

2. Trim the edges of the portraits with pinking shears.

3. Glue the portrait to the center of the colored construction paper.

4. Fold up each of the sides of the constructions paper along the pinked edges of the portrait.

5. At each corner, pinch the two sides to create a diagonal fold.

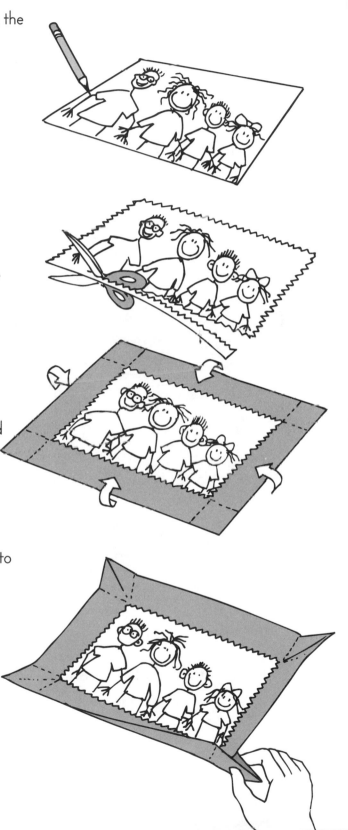

         Crafts for Young Children • EMC 720

Decorated Box

This little box makes a delightful gift.

materials

- small box with a lid

- paint (if boxes are shiny, tempera paint may not stick; use acrylic paint or spray paint instead)

- white glue

- decorations — buttons, macaroni, tiny shells, beans, ribbon

                   Crafts for Young Children • EMC 720

Steps to follow ➤

1. Paint the box. Let the box dry completely.

2. Glue decorations to the top of the box.

3. Allow at least a day for drying.

This box is a good place to store your favorite rock or found treasure.
Line it with Easter grass or shredded paper.

     Crafts for Young Children • EMC 720

Wreath of Hearts

Five friends each decorate one heart, then combine the hearts into a friendship wreath.

- patterns on page 78
- 5" (13 cm) squares cut from old file folders or tagboard
- 5" (13 cm) squares of pink construction paper
- 2' (61 cm) lengths of ribbon

- glue stick
- tempera paint
- sponges
- scissors
- Styrofoam meat trays
- hole punch

   Crafts for Young Children • EMC 720

Steps to follow >

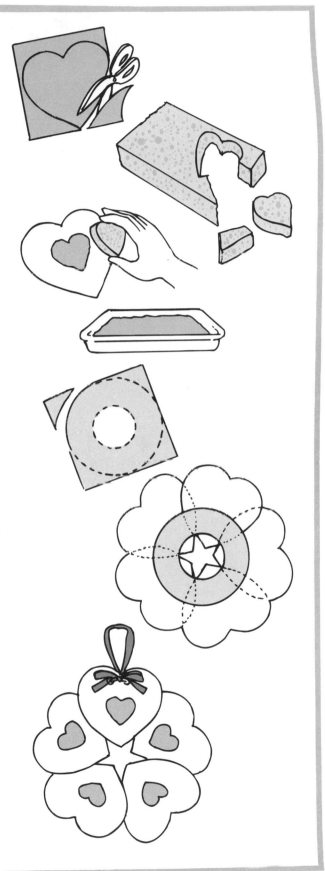

Making the Hearts

1. Make tagboard templates using the large heart pattern on page 78.

2. Cut heart-shaped sponges using the small heart pattern on page 78.

3. Each student uses a tagboard heart template to trace and cut a pink heart.

4. Pour paint into meat trays. Dip sponge hearts into paint and print on each heart. Let dry.

Making the Wreath

1. Round the corners of one tagboard square to form a circle. Cut a 2" (5 cm) circle out of the center.

2. Glue the hearts from five children around the tagboard circle. If you overlap them carefully, a star will form in the center.

3. Punch 2 holes about 1/2" (1.2 cm) apart near the top of one heart.

4. Run ribbon through the holes from the back. Tie into a bow on the front.

5. Hang heart wreaths by tying string, yarn, or monofilament line to the ribbon on the back side of the wreath.

Feathery Ducky

materials

- duck pattern on page 79
- 9" x 12" (23 x 30.5 cm) yellow construction paper
- 9" x 12" (23 x 30.5 cm) blue construction paper
- crayons
- paste or glue

Steps to follow ▶

1. Color the duck yellow and the beak orange. Color the eye black.

2. Cut out the duck and glue it to the blue paper.

3. Tear 1"–2" (2.5–5 cm) pieces from the yellow paper.

4. Beginning at the tail, paste one piece of yellow paper at a time to the duck's body, overlapping pieces slightly.

Tongue Depressor Mouse

Use this little mouse to help you tell a story.

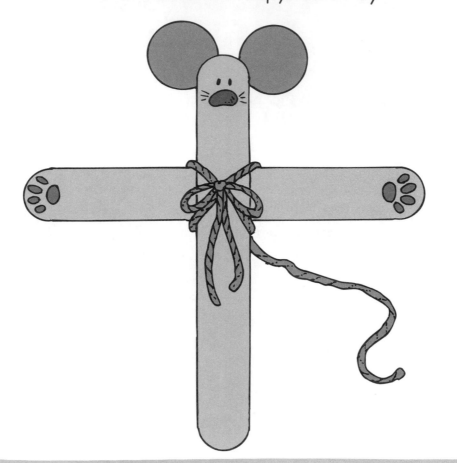

materials

- 2 tongue depressors
- 2 2" (5 cm) squares of brown construction paper
- 1 black bean
- 15" (38 cm) piece of black yarn
- fine tipped black marking pen
- glue

Steps to follow ►

1. Glue the 2 tongue depressors together as shown.

2. Round the corners on the brown paper squares to form circles.

3. Glue the circles to the back side of the top of the vertical tongue depressor.

4. Cut the piece of yarn in half. Wrap one piece around the juncture of the 2 tongue depressors. Tie a bow in the front.

5. Glue the other piece of yarn to the back for the tail.

6. Glue the black bean on as a nose.

7. Add eyes, whiskers, and paws with the felt pen.

Crafts for Young Children • EMC 720

Hungry Worm Weaving

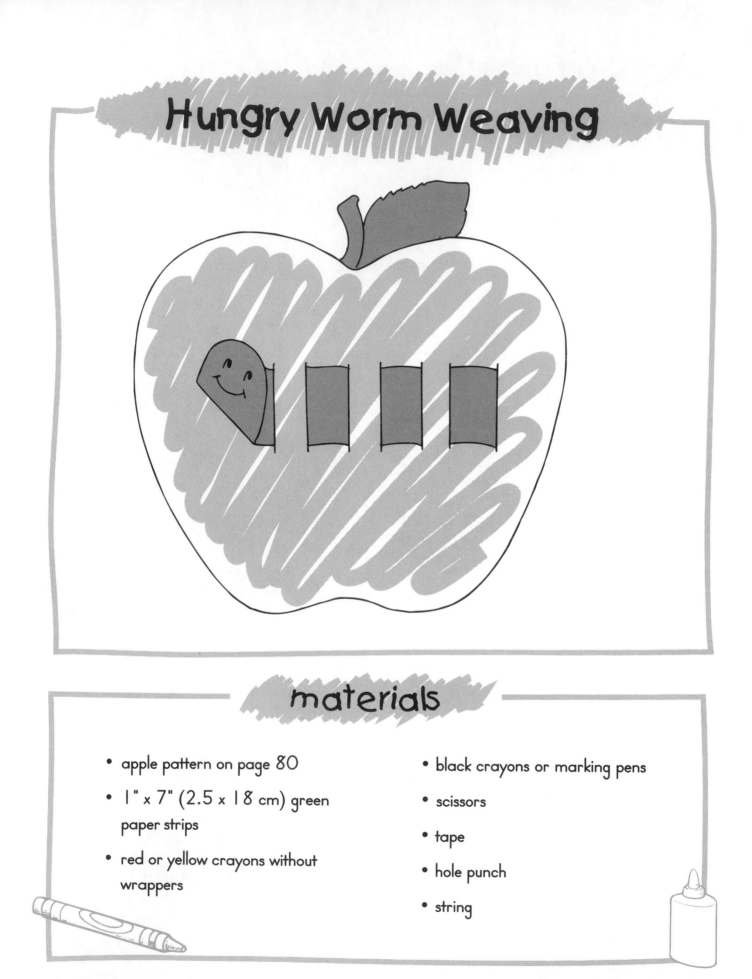

materials

- apple pattern on page 80
- 1" x 7" (2.5 x 18 cm) green paper strips
- red or yellow crayons without wrappers
- black crayons or marking pens
- scissors
- tape
- hole punch
- string

70

Steps to follow ►

1. Color the apple by rubbing the side of the unwrapped crayon across the apple.

2. Cut out the apple.

3. Fold the apple on the line and cut on the cut lines as shown.

4. Round one end of the green paper strip.

5. Weave the strip through the slits in the apple. Start on the back side.

6. Tape the squared end of the worm on the back side of the apple.

7. Fold the rounded end back to make the worm's head. Add eyes and a smile with crayon or marking pen.

8. Punch a hole in the top of the apple and insert a piece of string. Tie the ends together and hang the apple.

     Crafts for Young Children • EMC 720

Template for String-painted Butterflies, page 4
Reproduce on tagboard and cut out.

Crafts for Young Children • EMC 720

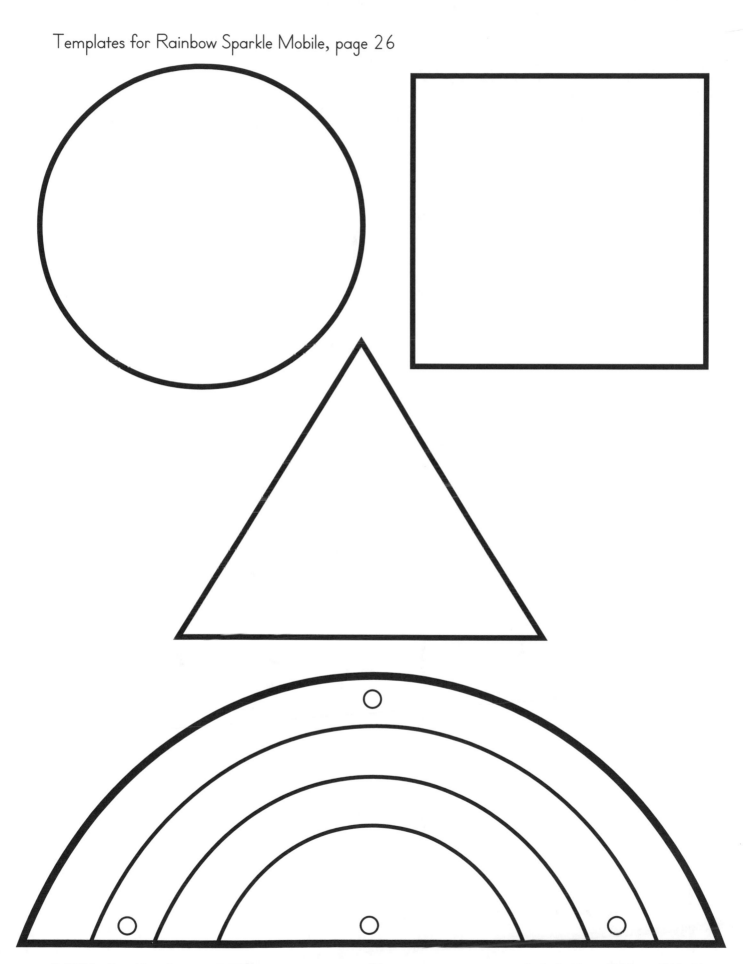

Crafts for Young Children • EMC 720

ear
cut two

Pattern for Box Puzzle, page 58

75   Crafts for Young Children • EMC 720

 Crafts for Young Children • EMC 720

Pattern for Box Puzzle, page 58

Crafts for Young Children • EMC 720

Pattern for Feathery Ducky, page 66

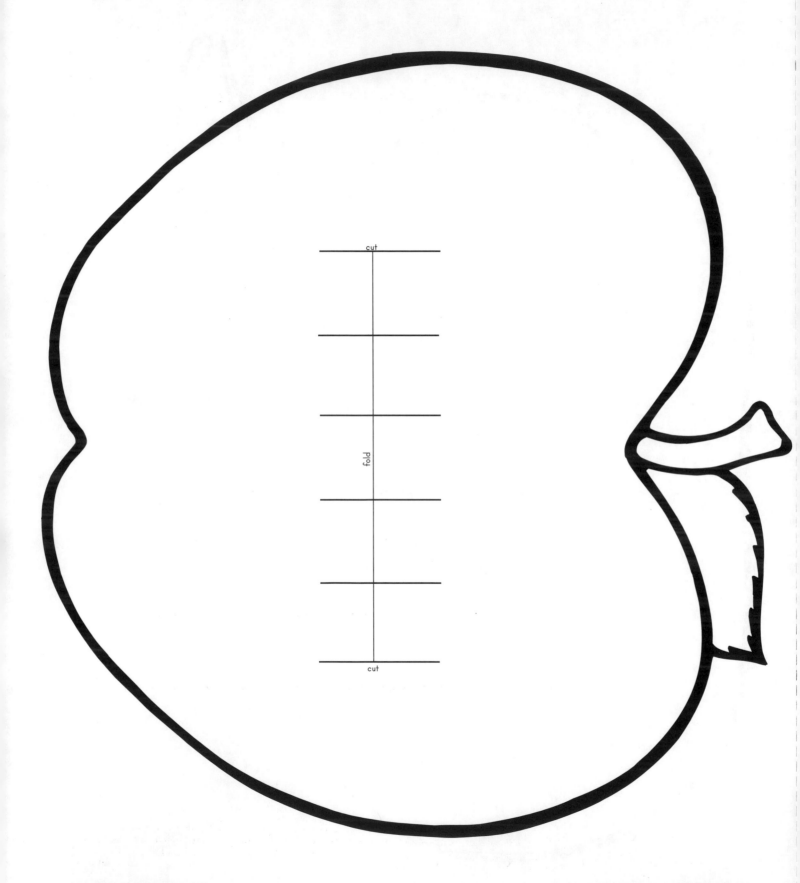

cut

fold

cut

Crafts for Young Children • EMC 720